THE ROOT

OF

BITTERNESS

EMMANUEL TWAGIRIMANA

THE ROOT

OF

BITTERNESS

EMMANUEL TWAGIRIMANA

An Imprint of ZionPearl Publishers

The Root of Bitterness

P.O.BOX 9437-00200
NAIROBI, KENYA.
Tel: +254722217710
Email:etwagirimana7@gmail.com

ISBN: 978-9966-8280-1-9

Published By:
ZionPearl Publishers
P.O Box 38670-00632, Nairobi-Kenya.
+254787907684
info@zionpearlpublishers.com
www.zionpearlpublishers.com

Dedication

To every person, young and old, who has once been offended or faced an injustice.

To the women of Eastern DRC (Democratic Republic of Congo), and survivors of sexual violence,

As you journey towards recovery, may God's Divine touch bring you holistic healing and restoration.

Table of Contents

Acknowledgements

Appreciations to ZionPearl Publishers, for bringing their contribution that allowed this work to get off the ground, your excellent expertise in editing, designing and publishing stands out. Thank you for your professional and kind help.

Our ministerial friends; I cannot mention all of you on this limited space. I want to register my appreciation to you for the numerous invitations and honor to speak and minister in your churches, conferences and crusades.

Special thanks to Felix Issachar Kanoti, Alphonse Yankulije, Daniel Kibarita, James Kamau and Felix Okojie for your labor with us in prayer. I am grateful for your tireless encouragement and support.

This book would not have been possible without the support of my wonderful wife Isabelle; She put in so much work in the writing and editing of the manuscript. I appreciate your companionship through it all. Your continuous encouragement is a great source of inspiration.

I want to thank my four beautiful children. Your fear for God and unquestioning obedience makes me very happy. I am always delighted to watch you grow and manifest God's greatness in you.

Lastly, I want to thank the Holy Trinity for grace, inspiration and guidance which has been the source and the reason for this work. Glory and Honour to you forever and ever.

Endorsements

A few days ago, Pastor Emmanuel Twagirimana told me about the book he was about to publish, a task which the Lord Jesus had commissioned him to do for the benefit of many who have been trapped in the root of bitterness. I thought that certainly the Lord is indeed interested in the condition of my own heart as much as anyone who will read this book. I understood that I must check my heart regularly and address, with the help of the Holy Spirit, whatever might be hidden deep within.

In 1999 while he was still recovering from the aftermath of the Rwandan nightmare and undergoing various treatments for his injuries, Pastor Emmanuel lived for nearly five months with my family in our home in England. And afterwards, we have visited each other many times. During those days, we heard him earnestly praying for everyone who has been harsh towards him and those who had been undermining his call and promises that in the near future God would use him to reach many nations.

Twenty years later, this evangelist who began so meekly is now a carrier of good news to the whole world. I firmly believe that it is his readiness to protect his heart from bitterness that has facilitated his partnership with the Lord, thus enabling him to effectively carry the good news to many nations, cultures and communities. Truly, this brother has become a well sought after speaker reaching out to those in low, middle and high classes.

Rev. Dr. Enoch Rubaduka

Senior Pastor of ICM, Ashford Pentecostal Church, UK.

In this book, Reverend Emmanuel Twagirimana, a man with an Apostolic and Evangelistic ministry is teaching us from his experience of SEVEN DAYS IN HEAVEN on how bitterness can damage someone's destiny and cause him/her to lose heaven.

Bitterness is among the less taught subjects in our modern time.

It remains the key factor of many disasters that we are facing in our society.

Every one of us has a fair share of it.

It is the root cause of rejection and wrong decisions taken by many.

It is like cancer, it imprisons.

It is considered as an auto punishment tool for other people's sins.

As you read the book you will learn:

- How to handle it
- How to close the loop on unresolved conflict by practicing forgiveness, love and joy

- How you can face the hurt and move forward in walking with the spirit
- How you can be healed and delivered from the damages caused by bitterness in your life.

Get it, read it and see how joy and hope will be restored to you.

Bishop Dr. F. Panga

Overseer, Jesus Touch the World International based in Congo and Kenya.

Foreword

The Almighty God, in His Wisdom, Might and Sovereignty has got a way of orchestrating events that transcend us. One of such many events in my life was when He brought across my path a man from the country of Rwanda. Although, I had been to the African continent on several occasions to share the Good News of the Gospel, I had never been to Rwanda.

I have been a church pastor for over 44 years in Vancouver, British Columbia. In those years, I had never met anyone from Rwanda. But as the Lord our God would have it, He orchestrated events that brought me into contact with a man from Rwanda, Emmanuel Twagirimana.

Emmanuel was introduced to me by those who had heard his testimony. Emmanuel was hit by bomb shrapnel during the Rwandan genocide that resulted into unspeakable carnage. When Emmanuel was hit, he died. Miraculously, this man came back from the dead after seven days. He documented the entire experience in his book entitled "Seven days in heaven".

Those that heard of Emmanuel's experience introduced him to me, and I invited him and his wife Isabelle to minister at Vancouver Native Pentecostal Church where I have been the lead pastor for over 20 years. Little did we know that Emmanuel's ministry to us at Vancouver Native Pentecostal Church (VNPC) would be used by the Lord as an opening to minister to many 1st Nations villages and communities around British Columbia, here in Canada.

After Emmanuel had ministered at our congregation, his compelling testimony led me to introduce him to several 1st Nations communities and villages. The decision to do this was not taken lightly. As an airline pilot, I have been trained to pay attention to details for the safety of the people and the aircraft entrusted to me by the airline. I had served as an elected chief in the Haida Gwaii nation for years and understood fully well the issues that affected my people.

Therefore, introducing Emmanuel Twagirimana to 1st nations communities and villages was weighed carefully, being fully persuaded that it would impact and alter the relational dynamics in our 1st Nations' communities and villages.

Emmanuel has been blessed with a unique perspective through his personal experience of the Rwandan Genocide, and the consequential impact of bitterness or inability to forgive those that have wronged us. His message resonated with our 1st Nations' people here in Canada who against their own will, were constrained to attend "Residential Schools" and were atrociously abused by those who were meant to provide education to them. Emmanuel's testimony was used of the Lord to enable him to address the issue of bitterness in the lives of the people in the earth.

His book is a warning to all of us, and every nation of the world to understand the destructive and deadly nature of bitterness. It is also a gift in pointing us to God's answer of forgiveness. As a 1st Nations' Canadian citizen, a local church pastor, an airline pilot and chief amongst my people, I recommend this book as one of the God given tools provided to us, to sort through the debris of bitterness and set us on to the path of forgiveness and love in CHRIST JESUS.

Bruce Brown

Senior Pastor, Vancouver Native Pentecostal Church.

Introduction

I wrote a book entitled SEVEN DAYS IN HEAVEN, and shared about my experience of death and restoration back to life after seven days. During the seven days in heaven, a lot was revealed to me.

I spoke in depth about the place of REST, which I was told while in heaven, that it's the place where people who have died in the Lord are found. While I was being shown around heaven, we reached this particular place and I saw many joyful people all adorned in white garments. The Lord Jesus told me, *"These are the people who served me faithfully, with pure hearts, love, and in holiness; they finished their work and are here to rest while waiting for others. Blessed are those who die in the Lord, that, they may rest from their labor, for their deeds will follow them."*

I saw Elijah, Enoch, Stephen, Peter and many others. As I looked around, I recognized some of the people with whom we had served God together, before the year 1994, but had died and we subsequently buried them. I was surprised to find them in heaven alive. They were even able to recognize me and talk to me.

However, there were other believers whom I expected to find there, but was surprised that they were not in heaven. This prompted me to ask Jesus, "My king, there are people I expected to meet here in heaven, but I haven't seen them. Where could they be? I am not seeing the treasurer (who was the custodian of the finances contributed towards the hospital ministry). I'm also not seeing the lady who coordinated the entire ministry's work. She was known for her zeal for God, love for people and her hospitable heart. They died, and we all thought they came to rest in heaven but, I am surprised they are not here."

Jesus responded and said to me, *"Those ones did not make it to the place of rest. The treasurer mismanaged the group's money, squandered it, then lied that it had been stolen from him. He left the world but his heart remained attached to it."*

The lady, on the other hand, could be compared to the people of Sodom and Gomorrah, whose hearts, despite leaving the two cities, still remained in that land. Incidentally, she fell sick and her friends abandoned her, with none of them paying her a visit during that time. She became angry and held on to bitterness, vowing never to forgive and let go of the offense in her heart. She fell out of God's grace and died a very bitter person, hence did not make it to the place of rest."

Unfortunately, many people in different nations, communities even some in churches hold on to bitterness and anger.

They are easily irritable, unforgiving, and carry grudges in their hearts.

Bitterness is a huge weight that weighs down many people all over the world. It is not limited to certain age groups, cultures, races, economic level, social status, or educational background. It is a major contributor to the destruction of marriages, it causes family breakdowns, friendship breakups and weakening of communities. It causes major health problems, leads to lack of productivity in the workplace, and leads to juvenile delinquency.

Some people, out of bitterness, direct their anger towards God. Others malign, insult and attack God's anointed servants and express bitterness towards them. Why do they do that? Because they don't understand God's ways.

Bitterness is a silent killer. It's a destroyer of marital destiny. Many marriages break up because one partner harboring bitterness against the other. Toxic relationships that are characterized by anger, emotional manipulation and other negative and hurtful feelings are on the rise. Instead of enjoying mutual support, many spouses find themselves trapped in toxic relationships. The same is true of relationships between parents and their children, bosses and their juniors, friends, siblings, and many other relationships.

Many victims of domestic violence or other forms of injustice develop emotional instability, anger, hopelessness and frustration. They tend to remain chronically angry, inward-looking, focused on the abuse they suffered, which makes them pick at their scabs.

Racism – the belief in the superiority of one race over another, resulting in discrimination and prejudice towards others, based on race or ethnicity – is another major cause of bitterness, historically.

People who have suffered injustice tend to harbor bitterness, which really is a form of unresolved anger. The bitterness gives rise to loss of hope, that the injustice or other moral wrong will be sufficiently acknowledged and addressed.

Unlike anger which easily shows on the outside, bitterness is deep rooted. It isn't easily recognizable. It does not easily manifest or bring to the surface symptoms that indicate that one has it. Many people are angry and hateful, but that's not what bitterness entails. Bitterness is an underlying problem that is not easily perceived; it dwells inside one's system. When it takes root, it causes defilement. This can take years or even longer periods of time. Hearts get defiled and then homes, societies, churches and whole nations.

The Bible says: *Pursue peace with all people, and holiness, without which no one will see the Lord: looking carefully lest anyone fall short of the grace of God; lest any root of bitterness springing up cause trouble, and by this many become defiled," (Hebrews 12:14-15, NKJV).*

I was prompted to write this book in order to expose bitterness, which is a scheme of the devil, and also to equip readers with the strength of a warrior, so they can live in the fullness of the joy of the Lord. People go through tough times and circumstances. For instance, the Rwandan nation was traumatized by a genocide that claimed the lives of close to one million people, in 1994. Many people around the world know of that tragedy. When it was all over, many believers who survived the genocide remained faithful to their call, but a good number developed bitterness and harbored pain for years.

The apartheid regime in South Africa left many victims living with bitterness. The pain they experienced was so deep, it caused them to pass over the bitterness to the upcoming generation. In my evangelistic missions in many countries across the world, I have witnessed the effects of bitterness in the lives of the people who harbor it.

One time while on a mission in Canada, I came across the indigenous inhabitants of the country. Many of them suffered historical injustices that left them nursing bitterness and pain.

In the course of my missions across the world, I have counselled many people trapped in the bondage of anger, unforgiveness, malice, jealousy and bitterness. This has helped me understand why God keeps urging me to encourage people to rejoice and be glad in the Lord each day of their lives. I have been directed to call people trapped in such circumstances to repentance. God revealed to me the secret hidden in JOY and LAUGHTER. I purposed to make it my daily prayer to God, to help me be joyful at all times. Joy is not only a weapon but a source of strength and a sign of gratitude. With joy, one is able to forgive and let go very fast. Any time I am preaching, I urge people to be joyful and to laugh; it's a way of resisting the devil, for he cannot live and thrive in a joyful heart.

The joy I am referring to in this book is divine, not the kind that is known by the world. Joy that is divine is hidden within, unlike the worldly joy that is evident and visible from outside. The joy that God gives resembles a spring of water which runs deeply underground! Other people may see the sufferings of a Christian, but they perceive not his inner joy. The joy that we experience as believers flows in us but comes from God, because we are connected to Him.

Worldly joy pleases the imagination, but it cannot satisfy the soul. The joy of God satisfies. Just as there is so much difference between a meal that is eaten and that which is painted on a wall, so is the difference between spiritual joy and worldly joy! Spiritual joy cleanses our hearts, turns us against sin, and infuses us with strength to stand firm and endure suffering. Divine joy helps us remain true to our calling even in the midst of heavy afflictions.

These are the last days. The Lord is cleansing and sanctifying His bride. His will and desire is that His bride makes herself ready, and be arrayed in fine linen.

And to her it was granted to be arrayed in fine linen, clean and bright, for the fine linen is the righteous acts of the saints. (Rev. 19:8).

As we embark on this journey, we will get a deeper understanding about the dreadful poison of bitterness, its effects on a person and how to uproot it from our lives so that divine, perfect joy may settle in.

Chapter One

THE ROOT

The Root

Everything that grows starts as a seed. A seed that is sown in the ground requires the right conditions to facilitate its germination. In instances where conditions are not right, it can stay in a dormant state even for years. But once conditions are favorable – the proper balance between light, darkness, moisture, oxygen and the right temperature, the seed sprouts to life. It starts taking in water and grows until the seed-coat splits apart. Then, air gets into the seed. The oxygen in the air helps the baby plant to burn the food stored inside the seed to produce energy, which the plant uses to grow.

Light, whether from the sun or an artificial source, say, a light bulb, gives the small plant the energy it needs to begin photosynthesis, which is the process of converting light energy into food. Once the roots are formed, they draw water from the soil and feed it to the plant. Like all living things, plants need water to survive. The roots grow downwards as the stem curls upward. As the plant keeps growing, its need for more water forces the roots to grow longer and stretch further to find the much-needed water from the soil. When these roots take hold and are firmly anchored in the soil, the young plant then emerges and anchored in the soil, the young plant then emerges and eventually breaks through the soil. When this happens, we say that the seed has sprouted. The scientific name

for this process is germination

A root is a source, or a bubbling fountain that is lying under the surface. Roots do not directly manifest or make themselves known, but are a source of nutrition or fuel for other elements that are on the surface. You don't usually see a plant showing off its root system, but if the plant didn't have a root system it wouldn't survived. A root's job is not to manifest on the surface, but to grow underground and fuel things that are on the surface.

The root of bitterness grows and develops the same way the roots of a plant develop in the soil. For the root of bitterness to form, it starts with a seed. This seed is deposited when someone or something offends you. Then, instead of forgiving and letting go, you hold on to the hurt and the offense.

The Bible instructs us to *forgive seventy times seven times a day*. When we fail to forgive, the offense gets stored in the heart and when subjected to the right conditions, it germinates and begins to grow. The Bible refers to it as a root, because it is hidden inside. Just like roots provide water for the plant to grow, in people, the root of bitterness develops and eventually leads to dire consequences.

Bitterness starts as a tiny little root underground, which is easy to hide and camouflage, making it very hard to detect. This root of bitterness is like cancer cells; it does its insidious work deep down in the marrow of a person's soul. Only after it has metastasized do symptoms surface through bitter words, thoughts, and deeds.

Those who are bitter will always hit on people without any reason at all, because they are just looking for anyone to relieve the bitterness on. Rarely would you find anyone admitting that they are bitter. They either deny or disguise it. A bitter person is hypersensitive, ungrateful, insincere, holds grudges and has mood swings.

Germination of Bitterness

The root of bitterness develops in certain conditions. Primarily, there must be a seed, soil and the right conditions for it to germinate, take root and grow. Bitterness in a person's soul is a hidden element that lies under the surface, and out of it springs up anger and other negative emotions against other people and against the circumstances around them. People who harbor bitterness get offended very fast by things other people do around them. It's like a brewing fountain that lies underneath, waiting to fuel something that is on the surface.

Looking at the story of Cain and Abel when they went to present offerings to God, it is clear that bitterness was at work in Cain, which led him to trouble. Abel's offering was accepted before God but Cain's wasn't, because it was given with the right attitude. Cain got so bitter, that even God warned him of the sin that was building up in his heart. Cain ended up killing his brother and, which made God to curse him [Cain].

Now Adam knew Eve his wife, and she conceived and bore Cain, and said, "I have acquired a man from the Lord." Then she bore again, this time his brother Abel. Now Abel was a keeper of sheep, but Cain was a tiller of the ground. And in the process of time it came to pass that Cain brought an offering of the fruit of the ground to the Lord. Abel also brought of the firstborn of his flock and of their fat. And the Lord respected Abel and his offering, but He did not respect Cain and his offering. And Cain was very angry, and his countenance fell. So the Lord said to Cain, "Why are you angry? And why has your countenance fallen? If you do well, will you not be accepted? And if you do not do well, sin lies at the door. And its desire is for you, but you should rule over it." Now Cain talked with Abel his brother; and it came to pass, when they were in the field, that Cain rose up against Abel his brother and killed him. (Genesis 4:1-8).

Cain expected his offering to be accepted, but it was rejected. Abel's faith made his sacrifice more excellent than Cain's. Abel's heart was right with God while Cain's wasn't. Cain took it that God had favored his brother, which made him visibly angry, because God had rejected his offering. Rather than repent and show humility and desire to change when God rebuked him, Cain responded with defensiveness, jealousy and bitterness towards his brother. Later, while in the field, he killed his brother. It started as a thought, which was admitted into his heart and flourished there. This thought developed and hatched into a terrible crime! It led to premeditated murder, caused by anger, jealousy, and pride. The root of bitterness was working in Cain.

From this story, we learn of the danger of harboring the slightest idea of bitterness, for we do not know how big it will eventually grow!

While warning him, God could discern that Cain's anger was rising to the point of danger, which, if not dealt with, would ultimately lead him to commit murder. Cain held on to his bitterness and jealousy, which finally prompted him to murder his brother.

The root of bitterness grows under the surface long before it gets detected.

Chapter Two

THE SEED

The Seed

All the plants we see, fully grown were once a seed.

Without seeds, there would be no plants. Since all roots must grow from a seed, there is also a seed that produces the root of bitterness. That seed is **offense.**

Offense is an injury or wrong done to a person. At the time a person gets offended, a seed is thrown and planted in the soil of his heart which can quickly spring up and germinate into a root of bitterness. Jesus Himself told us that it is impossible to avoid offenses; they come.

Then He said to the disciples, "It is impossible that no offenses should come, but woe to him through whom they do come." Luke 17:1 (NKJV)

Jesus was warning us and preparing us for what would happen in the future.

It is unavoidable to be offended at some point in our lives. Many experiences – false accusations, deceptions, betrayals, injustices, abuses – can push us into allowing the offense to enter our hearts.

When a person intentionally inflicts emotional pain on you, or insults and disrespects you, that can provoke you to anger. But it can also happen unintentionally, when someone does not mean to hurt you, but you get hurt in the process. Sometimes the hurt is only imagined; no one has hurt you, but somehow you feel that something wrong was done to you. The reality is, offenses do not cause bitterness.

Bitterness is a result of how a person processes the offense in his soul. At times, the enemy fuels thoughts that cause such a person to keep the offense in his heart. Once the seed of offense falls in the right and conducive environment, it germinates and develops into a root of bitterness, but if the conditions are not right, it fails to develop in which case it is quickly removed and thrown away. This is why some people become bitter while others do not, even though they experience the same offense.

When Jesus said that, *"Blessed is he who is not offended because of me" Mathew 11:6 (NKJV)*

He was speaking concerning John the Baptist because He perceived what was in John's heart and mind while he [John] was imprisoned. John's ministry had lasted a short time but it accomplished its mission of preparing the way for the Lord. God had demonstrated His power through John's preaching. Even Jesus confirmed that indeed, John was a godly man.

Among those that are born of women there is not a greater prophet than John the Baptist." Luke 7:28(NKJV).

Christ also identified John as the prophet whom Isaiah had talked about. He was the one who would lay a straight path before the Messiah, in preparation for His coming.

The voice of one crying in the wilderness: "Prepare the way of the LORD; Make straight in the desert a highway for our God." Isaiah 40:3 (NKJV)

On his side, John recognized Christ's divinity.

"Behold, the Lamb of God" John 1:29 (NKJV). And in Luke 3:22, He saw the Holy Spirit descend on Christ as a dove and heard the Father's voice declare Jesus to be His own Son. This happened when John saw Jesus coming towards him for baptism.

John lived his entire life in the wilderness (Matthew 3:4). When the Word of God came to him, He went around all the regions preaching repentance and remission of sins and baptizing. He did everything to fulfill God' calling on his life.

When he was put in prison, he began to doubt in his heart. No matter the anointing on him, he was still subject to all the feelings and passions common to man.

Then the disciples of John reported to him concerning all these things. And John, calling two of his disciples to him, sent them to Jesus, saying, "Are You the Coming One, or do we look for another?" Luke 7:18-19 (NKJV)

In response, Jesus sent John's disciples to tell him of the wondrous works of His ministry, as a confirmation to him that He indeed was the Christ. And Jesus added: *"Blessed is he who is not offended because of me."*

The devil tried to plant a seed of doubt in John's heart, to convince him that Jesus is not the Christ. He was drawing John's attention to what was happening to him, while he was in prison.

Often, when a person doesn't witness God's promises being fulfilled according to his plans, the enemy attacks his mind with questions about God's faithfulness, in order to rob him of his trust in the Lord. Such a person may end up questioning God's faithfulness. The enemy uses lies and deceptions to plant seeds of offense so as to make us question God's faithfulness, and to doubt His Word and the promises He has given us.

When a person believes that he is offended by God, the devil will proceed and pour into him unbelief, prayerlessness, lack of faith, regrets, and also make him impatient and anxious in regard to God's promises concerning his life, family, future, and ministry. The enemy's intention is to convince you that God is too slow, that He has ignored your requests and has left you behind. The enemy wants to bring you to the point of giving up your confidence in the Lord. That is what he wanted to achieve in John the Baptist.

Bitterness results from failure to properly respond to offenses. It is like an infection, which comes from the failure to properly attend to a wound.

Bitterness will grow in the soil of selfishness and self-centeredness. For example, maybe some people wronged you, or you suffered rejection perhaps in your childhood or in a friendship or in a marriage relationship; if you focus on yourself instead of focusing on God, you will become bitter.

Negative reaction to the instrument that caused the wound will not prevent the infection of the wound.

A friend of mine started a project in partnership with his friends. He was the visionary and founder. His friends were in charge of the legal aspects to ensure the project was registered and operational. When everything was done and ready, they legally assigned themselves executive roles. This man felt that he didn't get his rightful role as the founder, because he was assigned a much lower position. He shared with me how painful and frustrating it was for him. He felt betrayed. We prayed against the spirit of bitterness taking root in him and refused any negative emotion as a result of that act of betrayal. After the prayer, he confessed that he felt that God had healed his heart. He forgave the brothers and released them from his heart and has never felt the urge to confront them. He accepted to function in his assigned position. Years later, God elevated him, and he was able to do greater things than what he had planned earlier.

Prayer

I surrender to you oh Father, so that I may discern all offenses thrown to me and respond to them wisely and not bitterly.

Chapter Three

THE SOIL

The Soil

Germination of any seed requires that the conditions around it to be ideal. The soil has to be the right type with all the required nutrients and moisture levels to allow for germination and development of the seed. The heart is the soil of the seed of offense. Here we are speaking about the spiritual heart, which is the essence of who a person is. It is his authentic self where all dreams, visions, desires and passions live. It is the heart of a person that connects him to God.

Above all else guard your heart for it is the wellspring of life. Proverbs 4:23 (NKJV).

The heart is the wellspring of life; it

overflows into thoughts, words and actions. The spiritual heart is the most important part of a human being. It is considered the deepest area of a man's being.

It is the throne room of the spirit. This is important to note, because in our spirit, we find meaning and purpose in life. It's through the spirit that we have communion and fellowship with God. Through our spirit, we get intuition, which helps us discern between right and wrong, or good and evil. I may believe something in my **mind** and never respond, but if I hold the belief in my **heart**, then I will begin to act in ways that are in line with my heart's belief. The heart determines the outcome of one's life. Whatever it is that the heart is full of spills over and manifests in one's life.

If a man's heart is full of good things, goodness will flow out of it. But if the heart is full of sinful things, their life will manifest accordingly. It is not possible to live a life that is different from what is in his heart. You can only pretend for a short while but eventually, your heart will gain reign over your life and dictate your actions and decisions. Other people will know the contents of your heart through your words and actions.

Blessing or grief in life depend on how one rules and trains the heart. If a person directs and instructs their heart with godly input, there is no limit to their potential success before God and men. In the same breadth, if the heart is quickened and sanctified by the grace of God, the man will live a life of faith and holiness on earth, and enjoy everlasting life thereafter. If the heart is right, the actions of that person will also be right, for they are regulated and dominated by it. The heart is the seat of the Lord God, and the streams of spiritual life proceed from Him into the heart and all faculties of the soul.

The seed of offense planted in a person's heart may or may not germinate, depending on the conditions of the heart. It is the heart's condition that determines whether an offense will grow or not.

Have you ever wondered why two people suffering from the same offense respond differently? One becomes bitter, while the other outgrows it and becomes better. One becomes paralyzed while the other becomes empowered. In one, the heart was susceptible to infection, while in the other, the heart's immune system enabled them to sustain the wound and heal quickly. There may be scars but no wound, pus or infection. Offense sown in a heart that is submitted to the Almighty God, richly supplied with God's word and full of fire to do God's will, cannot take root.

The heart is deceitful above all things, and desperately wicked; who can know it? Jeremiah 17: 9 (NKJV)

It is only God who knows our hearts fully.

Our hearts, our inner beings, are far from perfect. We are born with a high inclination to sin and are easily deceived, blinded and trapped into sin. When we downplay our sin and fail to recognize that it is treason against God, we deceive ourselves. When a person has no strength to control his heart, he will be deceived and allow offense to stay in his heart longer than it should. A person may be offended in different ways leading to formation of resentment in his heart. Such a heart will harbor hostility and refuse to deal with the hurt through God's grace.

Successful war against bitterness depends on the level of enlightment and character of the person in question. If the person does not stand firm and guide the heart to forgive and let go, they cannot be able to overcome. The devil then takes advantage of this to spread destruction. Once the poison has been planted in the heart, it germinates and begins to grow. The longer a person keeps that offense or hurt in their heart, while lending ear to the voice of the evil one, the more their heart becomes an ideal ground for germination, and the root of bitterness develops. Thus, offense affords Satan an opportunity to cause destruction.

Bitterness takes root in the heart, growing deeper while staying hidden from view. With a bitter heart, the mind begins to form thoughts of anger, revenge, and grudges. These then become the hook that Satan uses to trap the person.

Many people carry bitterness in their hearts, which manifests in ways such as hate, racial and ethnic injustices, and wrangles, among others. The world is full of people who have not dealt with hurt they suffered earlier in life. They look for things to criticize, people to blame, and ways to justify their feelings. They know how to push hot buttons to gain a reaction in a way to further justify their bitterness.

A good man out of the good treasure of his heart brings forth good; and an evil man out of the evil treasure of his heart brings forth evil. For out of the abundance of the heart his mouth speaks.

Luke 6:45 (NKJV).

It is out of the overflow of the heart that the mouth speaks. It is not what goes into a man that makes him unclean, but what comes out of him. A good man brings forth kindness, gentleness, compassion, while an evil man brings forth bitterness, harsh surmises, and uncalled for condemnation. If the heart has roots of bitterness, it will without a doubt manifest them, because the enemy has already devoured it and will only need a short time to oversee its full destruction.

Bitterness thrives and survives in a sour, self-centered heart, the size and nature of the offense notwithstanding. A bitter heart is the seedbed for disorder and every evil thing in the society today. However, a heart full of God's grace will quickly recover by taking those thoughts captive unto the obedience of Christ, and continue without resentment towards the offender.

Be alert and of sober mind. Your enemy the devil prowls around like a roaring lion looking for someone to devour. 1 Peter 5:8 (NKJV)

Submit yourselves, then, to God. Resist the devil, and he will flee from you. James 4:7 (NKJV)

Create in me a clean heart, O God, and renew

a right spirit within me. Psalms 51:10 (NKJV)

Prayer

Give me strength Holy Father to guard my heart and direct it to you whenever I hurt, so that I may always triumph over the enemy.

Chapter Four

BITTERNESS

Bitterness

Once the seed of offense has been planted in the heart, nurtured to germinate and grow in supportive conditions, what follows is a process of destructive poisoning that is coordinated and accomplished by the devil.

Satan's great desire is for believers to FALL SHORT OF THE GRACE OF GOD.

"Falling short of God's grace" means "missing out on" God's grace, nullifying the grace of God or falling from grace. It is the worst situation a believer in Christ can get into. When one falls short of God's grace, bitterness keeps the grace of God away from their life.

The root of bitterness is one of the indications of a life short of God's grace.

Be careful that no one falls short of the grace of God, so that no root of bitterness will spring up to cause trouble and defile many. Hebrews 12:15(NKJV)

Grace is the divine power, divine life and ability that flows through us from God. God's word has many examples which show what God provided by sending Jesus to the cross.

The saving grace of God manifests itself through our will and works.

For it is God who works in you to will and to act on behalf of His good pleasure. Philippians 2:13 (NKJV)

Grace shows how God's ways and thoughts are different from human ways. He pours his empowering grace to whom He chooses.

But God has chosen the foolish things of the world to put to shame the wise, and God has chosen the weak things of the world to put to shame the things which are mighty; and the base things of the world and the things which are despised God has chosen, and the things which are not, to bring to nothing the things that are, that no flesh should glory in His presence. But of Him you are in Christ Jesus, who became for us wisdom from God and righteousness and sanctification and redemption that, as it is written, "He who glories, let him glory in the LORD." 1 CORINTHIANS 1:27-31 *(NKJV)*

The **grace** of God is publicly seen in believers.

By this all will know that you are My disciples, if you have love for one another. John 13:35 (NKJV)

The **grace** of God gives strength to endure suffering, increases joy in the Lord and sanctifies us.

My brethren, count it all joy when you fall into various trials, knowing that the testing of your faith produces patience. But let patience have its perfect work, that you may be perfect and complete, lacking nothing. (James 1:2-4).

A person who has fallen short of God's

grace is in a weak position and cannot exhibit God's power. Bitterness puts him in a perpetual, irritable state of mind that keeps him in animosity, inclining him towards harsh and uncharitable opinions about others.

Bitterness is unpleasant, angry, hostile, sour, and resentful. Its core is negative thoughts and emotions towards another person which occurs when a person refuses to forgive, let go and receive God's comfort.

The word "bitter" relates to something that is pungent, acidic, piercing, sharp, bitter or biting.

Bitterness is the emotional state where a person is hurting and angry. It is like a plant that has been incubated over time, which begins to draw energy underground, continually feeding on negative thoughts and emotions. Bitterness is not an emotion we are born with; rather it is something we pick and cultivate along the way. It brings no pleasure, it is unattractive and causes repulsion.

The root of bitterness keeps developing until it springs up. It may take a short time or even years. If not repented, it eventually springs up.

As long as there is a root, there will be fruits. They cannot be hidden forever. Bitterness does not have barriers; it is a spirit that can attack both Christians and non-Christians. It is a sign of falling out of God's grace.

The more you tread along the bitter path, the more firmly embedded in your life it becomes, and the less likely you are to consider a different way of thinking. Once bitterness takes root in our lives, it can be very difficult to root it out.

Bitterness is a deadly poison that brings pain to the heart, mind and body. If one's heart is full of bitterness, he is subject to living under the pain of hurt. Bitterness leads many people into spiritual, emotional and even physical bondage, defilement and countless sicknesses and diseases.

Bitterness is a key that opens doors for evil spirits. We earlier referred to Cain and

Abel. The anger and resentment that took root in Cain's heart became open doors for demonic entrance and activity. Sin (evil spirit) crouches at the door of the soul (the mind, will and emotions) like a vicious animal ready to spring through an open door, set up strongholds, and devour. Once the sin of bitterness opened the door for resentment and jealousy, the combination culminated into murder. Scripture explicitly states that anger (generated from bitterness) will always be accompanied by a spirit of murder.

Whoever hates his brother is a murderer, and you know that no murderer has eternal life abiding in him.

1 John 3:15 (NKJV)

I know a certain lady whose husband was physically and emotionally abusive to her. She was really offended, she would break out in tears at the memory of what her husband made her to go through.

She became bitter and plotted to take revenge against him. She decided to engage in a secret sexual affair which led her to commit adultery. This caused their marriage to get worse. Life became unbearable for them; they were faced with numerous financial challenges. The devil was attacking them from all sides because of her bitter heart. The anger and bitterness they held against each other created an avenue for the devil to bring destruction to their family. The situation kept getting worse but they came to their senses and repented, and their marriage got healed and restored.

Evil spirits thrive on bitterness. It's a wide-open door for them to move into the lives of people and cause them to fall into spiritual, mental or physical bondage. Once the devil has gotten an avenue, he comes in and causes havoc by stealing, killing and destroying. A person starts acting and reacting bitterly, and the word of grace in his mouth disappears.

Individuals who have allowed bitterness to take root in their hearts, get upset easily by circumstances around them, as they tend to view those circumstances as the source of their problems. Instead of forgiving and letting go, they allow these things to pile up and devour them from inside.

Bitterness is a disease that is associated with fellow human beings. We don't hold on to bitterness towards rain that does not fall at the right time, neither do we cultivate bitterness towards natural disasters. Rather we focus our bitterness (negative thoughts and emotions) towards fellow human beings whom we perceive to be the cause of pain or injury in our lives.

Bitterness fractures and weakens the soul and leads a person in the way of destruction. It blows out the candle of joy and leaves the soul in darkness. If a person allows bitterness to thrive in them, it damages the relationship they have with God and robs them of the joy of salvation. They become cynical, depressed, and miserable.

Cain became angry because God accepted Abel's sacrifice but rejected his. Anger and jealousy overcame him leading him to murder his brother. He was under the influence of the devil. Cain did not conquer his feelings toward his brother but harbored ill-will in his heart until it grew into a monster that pushed him to end his brother's life.

I know of people who drowned in alcoholism, drugs and substance abuse because of bitterness in their hearts. Some of them succumbed to premature deaths, while many led fruitless lives. Bitterness in the heart is like cancer in the body. A little undetected symptom will soon be deadly if not dealt with. It will cause trouble emotionally, physically, relationally and spiritually.

Prayer

Search my heart, oh Father, and enable me to abolish any form of bitterness in my heart. Remove every poison of bitterness from my past. Shut all doors that I may have opened to the enemy when I was bitter, which might have let in deadly consequences.

Chapter Five

Manifestation of the Root of Bitterness

Manifestation of the Root of Bitterness

Let all bitterness, wrath, anger, clamor, and evil speaking be put away from you, with all malice. Ephesians 4:31 (NKJV)

These six things the LORD hates, yes, seven are an abomination to Him: A proud look, a lying tongue, Hands that shed innocent blood, A heart that devises wicked plans, Feet that are swift in running to evil, A false witness who speaks lies, and one who sows discord among brethren. Proverbs 6:16-19 (NKJV)

But now you yourselves are to put off all these: anger, wrath, malice, blasphemy, filthy language out of your mouth. Colossians 3:8 (NKJV).

The root of bitterness manifests itself in different ways, the devil's intention being to keep us from living the kind of life that God intends for us. It is an emotion that affects an individual as well as whole groups of people. Bitterness has a destructive nature and produces bad fruits.

Fruits reveal the kind of tree we are. Though it may take time for the harvest to come, eventually the good or bad fruits of our lives will be evident.

When evil resides in the heart, it will be exposed in perverse speech and language that is contrary to the truth or love of God. If the root of bitterness is not quickly removed, it will eventually become a full-blown tree that produces bitter, wounding, and hurtful fruits for everyone who eats of it.

A good man out of the good treasure of his heart brings forth good; and an evil man out of the evil [a]treasure of his heart brings forth evil. For out of the abundance of the heart his mouth speaks. Luke 6:45 (NKJV).

The words we speak reveal what is in our hearts. If there is good treasure in the heart, it will be manifested; if evil, that too will show in due time. Our words say more about us than what we think, and go on to reveal those who are good or evil.

Bitterness is deeply destructive. It carries along excessive desire for vengeance as a result of deep resentment. It's ranked first among the list of things that grieve the Spirit of God.

Psychologist Dr. Carsten Wrosch has studied bitterness for fifteen years. He said that when harbored for a long time, bitterness may forecast patterns of biological dysregulation (a physiological impairment that can affect metabolism, immune response or organ function) and cause physical disease.

The most "troubling" fruit of the root of bitterness is unforgiveness!

Unforgiveness is failure to forgive those who have offended you. Unforgiveness hurts, keeps the pain alive, imprisons and shackles you to the past. It hinders our fellowship with God.

Unforgiveness, more than anything else, gives Satan advantage over us! When we allow germination of the seed of offense into a root of bitterness, it starts a very destructive work within.

For to this end I also wrote that I might put you to the test, whether you are obedient in all things. Now whom you forgive anything, I also forgive. For if indeed I have forgiven anything, I have forgiven that one for your sakes in the presence of Christ, lest Satan should take advantage of us; for we are not ignorant of his devices. 2 Corinthians 2:9-11 (NKJV).

Satan's knows that unforgiveness hinders our faith. He knows that God will not forgive our sins if we don't forgive other people.

For if you forgive men their trespasses, your heavenly Father will also forgive you. But if you do not forgive men their trespasses, neither will your Father forgive your trespasses. Matthew 6:14-15(NKJV).

Wrath

This is the inner burning and turmoil that explodes outwardly. It is the act of being sinfully and physically angry and indignant. Wrath is a demonstration of the loss of control, failure to rule self, failure to exercise restraint and manage emotions, which results in wicked deeds.

Whoever has no rule over his own spirit is like a city broken down, without walls. Proverbs 25:28(NKJV).

Holding on to past offences and hurts allows bitterness to alter your character, shifting your self-image from a competent and purpose-driven person to a helpless, irritable victim. Bitterness can make a person become self-protective, lose temper, have negative thoughts about the world, and waste opportunities and relationships that could have been fulfilling.

An angry man stirs up strife, and a furious man abounds in transgression. Proverbs 29:22 (NKJV).

Bad deeds and transgression always follow wrath.

Anger

This is a strong emotional reaction of displeasure, often leading to a strong desire for revenge or punishment.

Cain's anger would have been turned to good if he had repented and offered an acceptable sacrifice, but by nursing his anger against a holy and righteous God, he ended up committing murder.

Research has shown that anger affects a person in all ways, and is perhaps the most self-destructive emotion someone can inflict on themself. Chronic anger puts a person on a fight-or-flight mode, which gets hard-wired into the brain, and which can affect a person's health by bringing numerous changes in heart rate, blood pressure and immune response. These changes increase the risk of depression, heart disease and diabetes, among other conditions. Extreme anger has been shown to cause breast cancer in women.

"Predictably, chronic anxiety produces excess adrenaline and cortisol, which deplete the production of natural killer cells which is your body's foot soldier in the fight for cancer," noted another researcher named Dr. Michael Barry.

Anger can therefore cause premature death as well as aging faster through the wear-and-tear effect of stress hormones on organ systems. Anger is a robber of good health, peace of mind and youthful, good looks.

Clamor

This is the cry of strife, shouting in arguments, evil speaking or slander. It is a sign of no peace. It is loud and disturbing.

This is an accusation maliciously uttered, with the purpose or effect of damaging the reputation of another person.

It is a manifestation of bitterness in the heart.

Slander

This occurs when someone speaks falsely about another person, the end result being, either intentionally or unintentionally, that the reputation of that person gets damaged. When it happens, it becomes a divisive, discouraging and confusing weight that proves heavy to bear.

Malice

This is the propensity of inflicting injury upon another person, or to take pleasure in his misfortunes, being evil-minded or harboring feelings of intense hatred.

This kind of attitude is sensual and devilish in its influence as it is a deliberate attempt to harm another person. *"Every form of malice"* must be put off.

People express malice towards people they hate. It is one of the most dangerous fruits of bitterness.

Hatred

This is the fore-most danger that confronts us when we succumb to bitterness and allow it to rule our hearts by inflicting intense dislike of another. Hatred is distinct from short-lived feelings of animosity that may only manifest briefly and mildly.

Hatred is a form of active, ongoing hostility that often requires significant amounts of emotional energy. If hatred persists, it leads to a desire for revenge or pre-emptive action against a perceived threat. Some people harbor hatred for others but never act on it. Others become energized by hate and express their feelings through violent acts.

Hatred stirs up strife, but love covers all sins. Proverbs 10:12(NKJV).

In a few cases, a child of God is allowed to hate – when hating evil (Psalm 97:10), hating the assembly of evildoers (Psalm 26:5) and hating falsehood (Psalm 119:116); but he is urged to walk in love, to love his neighbor unconditionally, without prejudice. Poison isn't always something that you eat or drink; it can be an emotion. Hatred is a poison that is damaging and mind-consuming.

Hate affects our mental and physical health in a negative way. Conditions like insomnia, weight gain, depression, bad dreams, chronic illnesses and terrible diseases like cancer may start with hate and bitterness, according to a study by Greer and Morris (1975).

Hatred can also cause restless and obsessive thinking, paranoia, affecting the nervous, mental, immune system. It is a deadly poison and is spiritually blinding.

But he who hates his brother is in darkness and walks in darkness, and does not know where he is going, because the darkness has blinded his eyes. 1 John 2:11(NKJV).

Clearly, bitterness robs its victims of the good things in life as it takes charge of their lives. Bitter roots destroy from inside out. It has been said that if cornered, a rattle snake can become so angry, to the point of biting itself. Bitterness operates in a similar manner in the lives of people. It makes one unable to properly worship and serve the Lord, because hate and holiness cannot dwell in the same heart. And without the latter, no one will see God.

Bitterness causes one to break the

commandment of love, because with bitterness lodged in your heart, you cannot exercise both agape (divine love) and brotherly love.

Halts Progress in Your Life

Bitterness keeps a person trapped in the past, prolonging the pain which hinders them from moving forward in life. It keeps a person from living in the present moment, and blinds them from seeing good things around them. It creates in them a murmuring and complaining attitude.

Wastes Time and Energy

People who are bitter usually spend a sizeable amount of their time replaying the event, retelling it, and spinning out "if only that hadn't happened" scenarios. This robs them of their time, energy and resources which are far more important than whatever was taken from them.

Affects Relationships

In life, it is normal to go through a rough patch. During such times, friends and family extend support to you. However, when a person chooses to obsessively complain or constantly talk of the experience they have gone through, eventually it becomes draining on the listeners. Bitterness can drive away people who care about you while at the same time creating room for those who are bitter to come into your life. Many marriage relationships end up in divorce because of bitterness.

Bitterness Defiles Others!

Bitterness starts as a seed and grows into a huge tree that eventually defiles a person. Ultimately, it brings destruction to the individual's life before it destroys others.

In the medical world it is a known fact that certain diseases are infectious and can be contracted by others. They are called contagious or communicable diseases. There are numerous ways through which these diseases are spread but the bottom-line is, one can contract a disease from another person. Bitterness is one of those spiritual diseases that can be spread to many.

Defiling is tainting or contaminating. A bitter person is not content to keep his or her negative thoughts and emotions to himself/ herself. By their words and actions, a bitter person passes those negative emotions to others.

Bitterness is probably the number one peace-buster. It defiles and makes people unclean on the inside.

In Deuteronomy 29:18, Moses referred to it as *"a root bearing poisonous fruit and wormwood."*

Bitterness can spread in a whole community. A man can infect his wife, who in turn infects her children. The bitterness spreads, and soon the whole community gets infected.

Prayer

Lord God, I know that all anger, malice and hatred break my fellowship with you. I confess and repent from my bitterness and I believe that you are faithful and just to forgive, to root out all that is not pleasing to you from my heart and to cleanse me of all unrighteousness. I receive your forgiveness in Jesus name, Amen.

Chapter Six

UPROOTING BITTERNESS

Uprooting Bitterness

Life in one way or the other can lead us to face certain circumstances such as rejection, injustice, or an offense that can leave us angry and hurting. A person might get deeply offended in such situations to a point of becoming bitter. However, it's important to note that it's a personal choice to remain offended, for one can decide to overlook the situation and refuse to get offended. If a simple offense if not addressed, it develops into a bitter root.

Bitterness is slow and sneaky, and it can be vicious and destructive. If left unchecked, it inevitably destroys internal peace, contentment and happiness.

Controlling our angry responses and attitudes towards people is not enough; it is like pruning the branches of an overgrown plant, which still does not stop the plant from growing and developing other branches. To effectively deal with bitterness, one has to go beyond the visible fruits and dig deep into the ingrown roots, pluck them and throw them out.

Do not be overcome by evil, but overcome evil by good. Romans 12:21(NKJV).

Once you realize that bitterness has taken root in your heart, it is advisable that you first investigate what caused it, accept that indeed it is harbored inside you, and initiate the process of working towards uprooting and getting rid of it. Recognizing your struggle is the first step that shows that you are willing to let go of the bitterness in your heart. Repentance then follows, accompanied by faith that Jesus is willing and able to deliver and forgive you from the sin of bitterness. Once set free, you can rise above its effects and go on to be victorious.

Looking unto Jesus the author and finisher of our faith; who for the joy that was set before him endured the cross, despising the shame, and is sat down at the right hand of the throne of God. Hebrews 12:2(NKJV).

Decision and Repentance

The sin of bitterness will hinder many people from getting to heaven. No matter the extent of the offense, you are required to not let bitterness take root and thrive in your heart. If bitterness gains root in the heart, it gathers nutrients for its growth from the evil thoughts fed in the mind, and the root grows deeper. To uproot and overcome the root of bitterness, you need to realize and detect the struggle you have with it, recognize and accept that the root is in you, and accept the extent of its damage.

You must get to the point of making the decision to get rid of it. Repentance is a divinely appointed means of repairing the relationship between God and man. It is the first step towards uprooting and overcoming bitterness. It takes place when a person turns away from bitterness and comes back to God to find out what His will is concerning the offense that birthed bitterness. Do not allow bitterness to destroy you. Confess and repent of the bitterness in your heart so that the Lord can bring you to a better place of knowing Him.

Let the wicked forsake his way, and the unrighteous man his thoughts; let him return to the Lord, and He will have mercy on him; and to our God, for He will abundantly pardon. Isaiah 55:7(NKJV).

When a person is born again and filled with the spirit, he becomes a new creature in Christ Jesus. His mind gets renewed and quickened by God's spirit. However, that does not mean that he becomes sinless instantly, or mature enough to know and walk according to the will of God. Seasons of trials, and temptations, and weakness come, possibly causing the believers' life not to be in line with God's word.

If, as a child of God, you find yourself snared by the root of bitterness, you shouldn't think that it is the end of the world. Instead, you should quickly run back to the Father and confess.

Let us therefore come boldly to the throne of grace, that we may obtain mercy and find grace to help in time of need. Hebrews 4:16(NKJV).

Rise above the offense. Regardless of the intentions of others to try to offend you either through words, deeds or actions, take a firm stand and stay in charge of your mind and emotions. Make a deliberate decision to be a better person, focusing on your destiny. Pay no attention to the wounds that may have been inflicted on you and purpose to focus ahead, moving towards your destiny.

Look unto Jesus as the perfect example in regard to focusing on your destiny, considering that He harbored no offense against those who crucified Him. He chose to focus on His purpose and destiny. He is an author who finishes His work, the originator who took precedence in faith and is thus an excellent example for us to emulate.

He courageously bore and patiently endured the cross, despised its shame and willingly accepted to be crucified. As He hung on the cross, He exhibited an extraordinary amount of patience. He waited for God's purposes to be fulfilled in Him. He hung naked on the cross, despising its shame. The prospect of accomplishing the work that God had sent Him to do brought joy to His heart and gave Him the strength to overcome every obstacle ahead. That same joy has also been set before those who follow Christ, when struggling with sin, or when there is an opportunity to demonstrate faith. Each of us has a destiny to fulfill. When we learn to accept and forget the hurtful things that happen, we bar them from hindering our progression towards accomplishing our purpose. Constantly looking back and reflecting on the past keeps us from achieving our aspirations.

I challenge you to focus ahead, and look unto Jesus, who is our pace setter.

Walking in the Spirit

Then Peter said to them, "Repent, and let every one of you be baptized in the name of Jesus Christ for the remission of sins; and you shall receive the gift of the Holy Spirit. Acts 2:38 (NKJV).

After repenting from walking and acting in bitterness, the Holy Spirit takes over. At this point, uprooting the root of bitterness is solely His work.

Man is both a physical and spiritual being. The flesh is the physical aspect of man and is subject to being corrupted by sin. Natural senses, including desires and feelings cannot be completely eradicated, as long as one is still living in this physical and corruptible human body.

On the other hand, if you walk in the Spirit, you will do spiritual deeds. For the Spirit leads us to walk not according to the flesh. When filled with the Holy Spirit, He enables us to walk in accordance with His guidance and avoid the works of the flesh that lead many to destruction.

I say then: Walk in the Spirit, and you shall not fulfill the lust of the flesh. Galatians 5:16-26 (NKJV).

The manifestation of the fruits of bitterness falls under the works of the flesh. Lust is a strong craving or evil desire that comes with an overwhelming power that is almost irresistible. It comes with a passion that is unparalleled and almost impossible to defeat. The lust of the flesh is sin. Putting to death the deeds of the flesh is an act of not giving in to the cravings of the flesh. For the believer in Christ, this means using the power of the Holy Spirit to say **NO** to the desires of the flesh and refusing to respond to its demands. It takes the Holy Spirit, for He is the one that gives believers the power and conviction to say **NO**. If you walk in the Spirit, you will not give room for bitterness to grow in your heart. You will guard your heart to stay in perfect communion with God, which will cause you to bear fruits.

The Word of God and the Pursuit of Holiness

The Word of God is a weapon.

There is an extraordinary power in the Word of God that roots out the spirit of bitterness and fills our hearts with joy. This weapon works offensively on the physical, psychological and spiritual areas of our lives.

For the Word of God is living and powerful, and sharper than any two-edged sword, piercing even to the division of soul and spirit, and of joints and marrow, and is a discerner of the thoughts and intents of the heart. Hebrews 4:12(NKJV).

It is a double- edged sword that pierces, cuts, roots out and destroys the root of bitterness. Reading the Word of God, studying it, meditating on it, thinking about it, believing it, confessing it and applying it brings about healing of a bitter heart. It gives life – abundant life from the spirit within – to the physical body. It gives power to overcome, shapes our character and clothes us with heavenly beauty. God's Word can effectively separate the spirit and the soul, separate our thoughts from those that come from the Lord, and cause us to start responding to circumstances in line with the Word of God rather than from our physical or emotional senses. That which is strictly of the soul is what comes from our own mind. Thoughts, impressions and words that come from our spirit are the ones inspired by God. Not only does the Word touch our spiritual part, it touches the physical part too, that is, the bone and marrow. God's Word goes deeper into our spirit to cleanse, sanctify and heal. The Word discerns our thoughts and intents and thus has an impact on our psychological part.

As mentioned in the preceding chapters, the root of bitterness starts from the heart, poisons it, then enters the thoughts and finally manifests outwardly. It defiles the mind and body (the marrow and bone), but the Word comes to nullify the fruits and effects of the root of bitterness. Therefore, it is vital to hide and treasure the Word in our hearts.

Your word I have hidden in my heart that I might

not sin against You. Psalms 119:11 NKJV).

The act of hiding the Word of God in the heart is an indication of treasuring and keeping it somewhere precious. We know that the heart is the control center of our whole being. Once the word is hidden in our hearts, it empowers us not to sin. In case an offense comes into our hearts, it finds grace and power in there and thus gets nullified. However, if a heart is already poisoned with the roots of bitterness, and a person takes the Word of God into the heart, it will cast the root of bitterness out of the heart since the two cannot dwell in the same place. The Word will then start storing up grace, power, joy and everything else that comes with the power of God.

Scripture says: *"Sanctify them by your truth. Your word is truth." John 17:17 (NKJV)*

God's Word is truth, accurate, and without error. Sanctification by the Word allows holiness and obedience to Jesus. It causes us to submit to God and by so doing, we progressively move towards holiness.

Therefore, it is an on-going process. Our pursuit for holiness must not only be dependent on the Holy Spirit; it should also be diligent, passionate and fervent because God commands it.

To be sanctified is to be made holy. In the process of being made holy, we are delivered from bitterness, for we cannot be holy before the Lord while being mean-spirited and bitter towards others.

Chapter Seven

JOY AND LOVE

Joy and Love

A person walking in the Spirit will be easily discernible by their fruits. The first and second on the list of the fruit of the Spirit are Love and Joy. They go hand in hand; you cannot love if you are not joyful. And when you love, it brings joy to your heart.

Joy

This is my favorite part. My slogan is **"Laughter for Twenty-Four Hours."** Those who have interacted with me during my evangelistic missions, and those who have visited with me know that before preaching a sermon, I always tell the congregation to greet and tell each other to laugh for twenty-four hours. I don't say it just to energize the people. I received a revelation from the Lord about the secret hidden in laughter.

When I was in heaven, I noted that the only constant and present emotion there was joy. Jesus received me with joy; He greeted me and I burst in laugher; the angels smiled and laughed continuously; their teeth were golden. There is no sorrow, no pain, and no tears in heaven. It is only joy, joy, and more joy.

Laughter, joy, and love brings into our lives a piece of heaven.

Some health practitioners have resorted to making use of *laughter therapy* to treat patients, especially those suffering from depression, stress and diabetes. Some people claim that laughter therapy reduces the cost of health care, and boosts the cardiovascular system's wellness. Laughter from comedy and entertainment is good, but it does not fix most inner problems, neither does worldly joy, but divine joy totally eradicates bitterness by its roots.

When I urge people to *laugh for twenty-four*

hours, It's the laughter from within, that which comes out as a result of the joy planted in the heart. It's not because everything is going on well, but because the heart is at rest and assured, and hidden in Christ. No matter the insults, or how big the offense comes to attack, no matter the situation, the heart remains on the defensive because of the joy in it.

A joyful heart is good medicine, but a crushed spirit dries up the bones. Proverbs 17:22(NKJV).

Joy is the complete opposite of bitterness. Whereas joy is sweet and light, bitterness is a poison that dries the bones. Joy is good medicine. A joyful spirit impacts greatly on the body, and contributes to its welfare. Joy is evidence of victory over Satan's poison of offense. Joy is a powerful weapon that casts out stress, anxiety and grudges. The devil gets mad whenever we choose to walk in joy, for he lacks the means to hit us with frustration in our joyful state. Therefore, we ought to maintain a cheerful heart, and not hold on to a broken spirit. The Lord told me to encourage the church to always be filled with joy. Constant joy from within neutralizes the root of bitterness, dries and completely kills it. The joy in a person's life is God's will, it is pleasing to Him. Our joy is fulfilled, when we are filled with the Joy of the Lord.

I am the true vine, and My Father is the vinedresser. Every branch in Me that does not bear fruit He takes away; and every branch that bears fruit He prunes, that it may bear more fruit. You are already clean because of the word which I have spoken to you. Abide in Me, and I in you. As the branch cannot bear fruit of itself, unless it abides in the vine, neither can you, unless you abide in Me.

I am the vine, you are the branches. He who abides in Me, and I in him, bears much fruit; for without Me you can do nothing. If anyone does not abide in Me, he is cast out as a branch and is withered; and they gather them and throw them into the fire, and they are burned. If you abide in Me, and My words abide in you, you will ask what you desire, and it shall be done for you. By this My Father is glorified, that you bear much fruit; so, you will be My disciples

As the Father loved Me, I also have loved you; abide in My love. If you keep My commandments, you will abide in My love, just as I have kept My Father's commandments and abide in His love. These things I have spoken to you, that My joy may remain in you, and that your joy may be full. This is My commandment, that you love one another as I have loved you. John 15:1-12(NKJV).

Jesus refers to His own joy as being in us. While pondering how one acquires the joy of the Lord, I read the Scripture above and got an answer.

Jesus put it to us that He is the true vine, and that we, believers, are the branches. As we studied about a tree from its roots to the branches, we got to understand that the roots absorb water and nutrients from the soil, dissolve and take them up to the stem, which transports those nutrients throughout the plant. Branches that have been perfectly connected to the vine receive full supply of water and nutrients and bear fruits.

The key to acquiring the fullness of the Lord's joy is STAYING CONNECTED TO HIM.

The joy of the Lord flows to the believer and in return the believers' joy is made complete. That way, the believer is enriched not only by his joy, but also by the joy of the vine. He enjoys what the Lord enjoys as he abides in Him. This kind of joy is what uproots bitterness by its roots, and puts to death all its fruits and consequences.

Joy makes it easier to keep God's commandment of **LOVE.** *John 15:12 (NKJV).*

Love

Love is exceptionally excellent. It's not arrogant or rude, does not insist on its own way or rights; it's not irritable or resentful. Love is never selfish, never quick to take offense, keeps no score of wrongs and does not take account of the evil done to it.

Love does not behave rudely, does not seek its own, is not provoked, thinks no evil. 1 Corinthians 13:5, (NKJV)

'And you shall love the Lord your God with all your heart, with all your soul, with all your mind, and with all your strength.' This is the first commandment. And the second, like it, is this: 'You shall love your neighbor as yourself.' There is no other commandment greater than these. Mark 12:30-31, (NKJV).

Loving our neighbor includes sharing with the poor and the alien; compassion and absolute honesty and justice in our relationships with others; impartiality; a refusal to be party to gossip or slander; an absence of malice toward anyone and a refusal to bear a grudge; taking care never to put another's life at risk and never taking private vengeance upon another.

This love is one of the greatest challenges in life; not only should you love those who are good to you, but also those who hurt and offend you. Among our neighbors are friends, enemies, and strangers. Neighbors include enemies, even when we'd rather draw back, ridicule or look the other way because of the pain they've caused us. Enemies are people in our lives who in one way or the other have caused us anger and frustration, they might have insulted, disrespected and abused us at some particular point in life.

There has been news across the world of children who have endured great suffering in the hands of their step parents, people whose reputation has been destroyed by rumor mongers and false reporters, leaving them feeling crushed or confused.

How can one who has endured such atrocities be able to express love? Love does not erase the fact that a person was offended, but bring sanity when offense or roots of bitterness want to grow in the heart of the victim. It empowers individuals to love those who have offended or hurt them in the present or the past and refrain from taking revenge or plotting evil against them. It brings healing and deliverance from bitterness.

One can learn to love their enemies through knowing and acknowledging God's love. Considering with seriousness the immense love of God to us, we should be compelled to love our enemies, and not allow bitterness to take root and grow in our hearts. Christ paid the price for our sins without our merit; by His grace we were saved. He took the load of our heavy burden, and forgave our wrongs, giving us freedom from Satan's captivity.

The thought of all the sins in our lives that Jesus has covered and wiped away should move us to extend grace to our enemies and make room in our hearts for the Spirit to work out forgiveness for them.

Root out bitterness by the love of God, AGAPE.

Agape is divine love; that selfless, sacrificial, unconditional love that shows concern for the welfare of others. It is the immeasurable, incomparable love which God unreservedly extended to humankind who were undeserving.

It is the highest type of love. God's demonstration of love led Him to sacrifice His Son, Jesus for the sake of His love for mankind. Believers' love should always be demonstrated by their actions. It should not be based on feelings but as a determined act of the will, a joyful decision to put the welfare of others above one's own. This kind of love does not come naturally to us, since humans in their capacity are incapable of producing such kind of a love. Loving people with God's love comes only from God, through the Holy Spirit.

This love is a fruit of the Spirit, and with it the root of bitterness is eradicated.

Love is very beneficial, wise, powerful, and gracious, it rises above offenses, affronts and insults.

A fool's wrath is known at once, but a prudent man covers shame. Proverbs 12:16 (NKJV).

The discretion of a man makes him slow to anger,

and his glory is to overlook a transgression. Proverbs 19:11 (NKJV).

Given the increasing anger and division in our society and the world in general, we should all learn to do with quite a bit more of *this kind of love*.

Chapter Eight

FORGIVENESS AND PURSUING PEACE WITH ALL MEN

Forgiveness and Pursuing Peace with all Men

At the start of this book, I told of a lady whom I thought I would find in the place of rest in heaven where all the saints are, but I did not find her there (Revelation 14:13). I was concerned over it and inquired from Jesus why she was not there. His response was that the lady died a very bitter person; she had refused to forgive friends who had deserted her when she was sick. She held on to unforgiveness up to the point of death. He equated her story to that of Sodom and Gomorrah.

Sodom and Gomorrah were places of

wickedness, inhabited by men who were exceedingly wicked and sinful against God. They displayed evil traits such as violence and homosexual acts, they were proud and rich, but did not do any charity work. They disregarded the poor and offered no help to the needy.

Look, this was the iniquity of your sister Sodom: She and her daughter had pride, fullness of food, and abundance of idleness; neither did she strengthen the hand of the poor and needy. And they were haughty and committed abomination before Me; therefore, I took them away as I saw fit. Ezekiel 16:49-50 (NKJV).

"But his wife, from behind him, looked back, and she became a pillar of salt." Genesis 19:26 (NKJV).

Looking back means *"to regard, to consider, paying attention to."* It is more than to glance over one's shoulder. What she chose to value in her heart led her to sin and eternal destruction. Like Lot's wife, who looked back at Sodom and Gomorrah and became a pillar of salt, this lady also looked back when she entertained unforgiveness and bitterness in her heart. She was offended badly and constantly relived the hurt, until she died.

Living with a sense of injustice or unfairness, and grumbling about those who have wronged you, hurts your soul. It carves out a place in you that won't allow healing. As I mentioned earlier, unforgiveness causes a person to relive the past, always chew on the bad things, the hurt, and the injustice that happened, which makes them lose focus of what lies ahead. It is like being imprisoned by the past, whereby the offense and the offender are still present in the mind; the details of the offence or betrayal, the words of insults that were hurled at you keep playing in your mind. The heart grows heavy and the pain pricks like thorns.

These vicious thoughts and harassing memories eventually result in anger and rage, to the point of entertaining thoughts of revenge. The lust of the flesh – Satan's open door – gains control and leads to more devastating sins and demonic activities. Where there is bitterness, unforgiveness is present too, and vice versa. Unforgiveness is a bad emotion and a dangerous sin. Unfortunately, many people hold on to it. It is stubborn. Once adopted, it is not easy to let go. It hinders our faith from working.

It's a sin that eats inside-out, like a growing cancer, hurting both the victim and other people, making it impossible for one to lead a victorious Christian life.

The mother of unforgiveness is bitterness, deeply rooted in the heart. This root destroys its own container. Unforgiveness can cause health problems such as mental depression, cancer and arthritis. Failure to forgive, if you are a believer, is proof that you do not cherish the forgiveness you have received through the blood of the Son of God. It is denial of its effectiveness and refusal to trust, embrace and treasure it.

If we desire the forgiveness of God for our daily missteps, we must be prepared to extend forgiveness to others for their missteps against us.

For if you forgive others for their transgressions, your heavenly Father will also forgive you. But if you do not forgive others, then your Father will not forgive your transgressions. Matthew 6:14-15 (NKJV).

Forgiveness involves the process of making a conscious decision to let go of negative feelings, whether the offender deserves it or not.

It's possible for God not to forgive your sins on earth for failure to forgive others. That is to say, that if you die unrepentant, you will stand before God unforgiven. The Bible speaks of the everlasting contempt, fire, punishment and destruction that awaits all those who reject God and His Word. The only way to the Father is through repentance, faith and trust in His Son, Jesus Christ, but without repentance, you will likewise perish.

Forgiveness calms stress levels, leading to improved health. It is a fundamental component of healthy relationships and overall well-being.

I had a conversation with my wife, Isabelle. We were talking about life in general, then narrowed down to issues in marriages. I was sharing with her about incidences of "cold war" in marriages. There are many homes that burn in the night and cool during the day. There are spouses who cannot tolerate each other or live together, hence end up divorcing.

As we talked (2016), we flashed back at our fifteen years in marriage; the tough things we have gone through together, raising our four children, believing to do exploits in our different callings and skills. We also admitted that sometimes, anger and quarrels got the best of us. During those moments, we embraced repentance and chose to root out any bitterness that could cripple our lives, and chose forgiveness.

Bitterness destroys marital unity. Disunity in marriage is very dangerous because it makes marriage itself lose its essence.

Traveling through nations and doing

evangelism has brought to me knowledge of people, communities and nations that have experienced hurt, offences and wounds, and are going through life with scars of what happened to them, or their ancestors.

I have listened to issues that have touched my heart as I seek to understand how far the human heart, soul or spirit can go and be able to forgive and move on despite the atrocities it has been subjected to. One would wonder where justice is. Is God turning a blind eye to every wrongdoing and injustice? Injustice has become widespread in the world today.

The '90's was a devastating time for the Great Lakes Region located in Central and East Africa. Millions of people were massacred and property destroyed. People ran away from the killers, hiding in forests and bushes without any hope for protection. Many families were wiped out, leaving only a few survivors whose memory is full of horrible stories of the genocide, massacres, rapes, theft and beatings. People from different tribes (in Rwanda, Burundi and Eastern Congo) went through a lot. Lots of tears and blood was shed in that region.

The question that followed was, *how can you reconcile with the person who massacred your entire family? How can you live together with a group of people whose members participated in the killings? How can tribes, ethnic groups who have killed each other historically come together genuinely and love one another?*

True reconciliation starts with forgiveness which is personal and internal. The offended person lets go of the hurt and grudge and moves on without the input of the offender.

In Democratic Republic of Congo, those decades of fighting have caused terrible consequences on the men, women and children. Many acts of violence in the forests of DRC have taken place, killings, beatings, rape, leaving some women infected with HIV/AIDS, shame and suffering, trauma, torture and forceful seizure of land especially if it is rich in minerals.

Gynecologist, Dr. Dennis Mukwege (Nobel

Peace Prize Winner, 2018), has dedicated his time, career and profession to try and repair the damage that has been inflicted on women who were brutally raped and sexually assaulted by soldiers and gangs. Dr. Mukwege runs Panzi Hospital in Bukavu, and has tremendously helped in the physical and emotional restoration of thousands of women.

After treatment, the women are provided with temporary shelter as part of rehabilitation. While on a gospel mission in Bukavu, DRC, in August 2018 at Fire Ministries Church, pastored by my spiritual children Pastors Safari and Deborah Buhendwa, Isabelle and I were privileged to visit Panzi Hospital, and witnessed the work that Dr. Mukwege has done for those victims. There were thousands of women, young and old, some in their temporary shelters, others hospitalized, some had already gone through surgery, others were still on the waiting list.

We did rounds in the wards where the

women were resting. One could see and feel the deep, physical and emotional agony these women had been subjected to. Isabelle was visibly holding back tears as the chief nurse explained to us the pain and suffering these women had gone through. In my mind, I kept thinking, *how much anger could they be holding on to? What would happen if they met those who raped them? What kind of injustice is this? Why would this kind of suffering happen to a human being?* I'm sure they felt contaminated, degraded, hopeless and alienated. I could not imagine how they were coping with the thought that they had lost control of their life, dignity and self-worth.

If you are a visitor at the hospital, you are not allowed to talk to those women. However, I felt that I could not leave that place without addressing them. I requested the nurse to grant me permission to do so. The room was big and had a capacity of approximately fifty beds, all of which were occupied. Some of the women were nursing babies who had been conceived during the rape atrocities against the women.

I was given two minutes to address them. I wondered what to tell them since from what we had been told, many of them were traumatized at the sight of men near them.

"Hi, I am Rev. Emmanuel Twagirimana and together with me is my wife, Isabelle," I told them. "We are also accompanied by our host here, Pastor Safari. I am a servant of God on a preaching mission to this city. Today, I was privileged to come and visit you."

I noted that they were paying attention, therefore I proceeded to encourage them.

"Be strong and courageous, because it is not over with you. Do not lose heart, though you have suffered a lot. Great help and healing are coming to you through the Lord Jesus. A time is coming when you will be healed and restored back to life. We love you and would like to pray for you."

They all gave us an okay to pray for them.

I then asked if any of them wished to receive

Jesus Christ as their Lord and savior. Those who could raise their hands did so and we prayed for them. Thereafter, I prayed for their quick and holistic healing and restoration.

Forgiveness is not easy. It takes time, it is costly when the hurt went too deep, or because the person was too abusive, or expressed no regret. There must be willingness to forgive. If we are willing, we will make a choice to forgive and, receive strength from the cross of Jesus Christ whereby we are empowered to forgive as God in Christ has forgiven us. At the cross we have been forgiven, therefore as we trust and believe in the work accomplished at the cross, we will easily forgive.

I was in South Africa in 2018 for a gospel outreach mission, and got an opportunity to visit the historic Morris Isaacson High School, which is widely known because of the Soweto uprising.

As we read from history, this uprising was on 16th June 1976, when Black South African high school students in Soweto went out on a protest march against the Afrikaans Medium Decree of 1974, which forced all black schools to use Afrikaans and English in a 50–50 mix as languages of instruction, though the students preferred English. The march was peaceful, but they were met with brutal police force and violence erupted, leading to shootings. A number of students lost their lives. One of the dead students was named Hector Pieterson.

We proceeded to visit a memorial site named in the name of the slain student, The Hector Pieterson Memorial. This place is dedicated to pay tribute to the victims of this 1976 Soweto uprising; a key event in the history of the struggle for South Africa's liberation. The memorial is a museum spread with placards, prints and broadcast pictures about how black people in South African suffered at the hands of the white oppressors during apartheid.

Apartheid was a system marked with a lot of segregation. Non-whites were not accorded the same rights and privileges as whites. Central to this racial class system was a set of racial categories invented by apartheid's architects: white, Black (African), Colored (of mixed racial heritage), and Indians (descendants from South Asian immigrants). The system segregated public facilities such as benches and drinking fountains, dictated where blacks and whites could live and work, what sort of jobs they could apply and, where and when they could travel.

Multiracial communities were destroyed, and African, Colored, and Indian people were forcibly removed from places designated for whites. Blacks were not allowed to run businesses or professional practices in areas designated as "white South Africa," unless they had a permit, such being granted only exceptionally. They were required to move to the black "homelands" and set up businesses and practices there. Transport, other services and civil facilities were segregated.

The concept of apartheid was predicated on

classifying "non-whites" as sub-human and white people as God-like – a superior race that could kill, rape, enslave and exploit without consequences. Women suffered both racial and gender discrimination. Jobs were hard to find. Many Black and Colored women worked as agricultural or domestic workers with extremely low wages. Children suffered from diseases caused by malnutrition and sanitation problems; mortality rates were high.

Apartheid affected the people psychologically, politically, socially, economically and mentally. The impact of colonial oppression, genocide and other kinds of mass atrocities were felt across multiple generations of descendants of survivors.

Apartheid has caused problems like poverty, racism and violence, psychological disorders, a generation of maladjusted children, trauma associated with growing up in a divided society, landlessness, economic exclusion, and barriers to decent education among other things. The pain and suffering that multiple generations of black South Africans lived through structurally and systematically, can still be evidenced today through young people. The youth believe that much like their descendants, they live a life of poverty because white people are uncompromising in their position to redress the injustices. There are feelings of resentment by black South Africans towards white people for the role they played during apartheid and their remorseless existence in the new South Africa. Stories told by parents to their children of the violence they experienced during apartheid can burden them with feelings of anxiety, resentment and possibly depression. Apartheid clearly created hate, social disorder and bitterness, and many other vices.

*Mpho Tutu and Desmond Tutu in their book "**Book of Forgiving**" (2014), mentioned that full forgiveness is when the relationship after is different from relationship before, and that has not yet happened in South Africa.*

In a case involving such injustices, forgiveness is a process that must be achieved with economic restoration.

In the year 2011, I visited Canada, and was excited to be told about the history of that country by my host, Daniel Kibarita. He informed me of the people I had never heard of before – the First Nations people.

In 2014, by invitation of Pastor Bruce Brown (Pastor at Vancouver Native Pentecostal Church), I was able to tour the reservations in Northern British Colombia, preaching the gospel. It was a delight for my wife and I to interact with the First Nations, and learn about their history. We flew from Vancouver to Prince Rupert then took a ferry that brought us to LaxKw'alaams, previously known as Port Simpson. We had a series of amazing meetings in Laxkw'alaams as well as mingle with the locals, who opened up to us about their past. They told us about abuses, beatings and rape experiences that they went through when they were taken into residential schools. For more than a century, tens of thousands of families were torn apart as children were kidnapped or forcibly removed from their homes. Residential schools were part of an extensive education system set up by the Canadian government and administered by churches with the objective of indoctrinating aboriginal children into the Euro-Canadian and Christian way of life.

The abuses many endured in residential schools have been passed down generationally. There were numerous cases of suicides for the survivors of the atrocities. Survivors and their descendants alike report difficulty forming good and trusting relationships with their spouses and family members. Children growing up without such trusting relationships often develop an inability to respond to stress without resorting to external stimuli such as destructive addictions. There is a connection between residential schools and the social problems among the First Nations today, like unemployment, domestic violence, and the over-representation of aboriginal children in foster care and the high homicide rate of indigenous women.

Forgiveness is possible. No matter the injury caused, forgiveness is good and vital. Sometimes when we count blessings around us, we find that every hardship has contributed to a good outcome in our lives. We can use those disappointments, hardships or injustice as energy to rise up and work towards a goal in life.

An individual can forgive and become a great advocate of restorative justice of the society or the whole community.

Jesus reminded me of two examples of forgiveness: when He forgave as He hang on the cross, and Stephen's forgiveness when he was being stoned.

Facing injustice and execution, Jesus prayed for His persecutors, accusers and friends who had deserted Him. Without murmuring, cursing or vengeance, He freely forgave all of them.

Then Jesus said, "Father, forgive them, for they

do not know what they do." And they divided His garments and cast lots. Luke 23:34 (NKJV).

Steven prayed for the forgiveness of those who were stoning him. He had courage and character.

Then he knelt down and cried out with a loud voice, "Lord, do not charge them with this sin." And when he had said this, he fell asleep. Acts 7:60 (NKJV).

By God's grace and help, you can do what seems humanly impossible to do; you can release that spiritual burden of unforgiveness. Forgiveness opens the prison door and sets you free from your past pain. It reduces the offender's grip on you and helps you focus on other positive areas of your life. It always results in healing, wholeness and restoration. With forgiveness, the Word of God becomes clearer, you are drawn nearer to God, and your heart is purified.

Jesus himself is seated on the mercy seat to forgive. He forgives every day, and wants us to forgive.

Chapter Nine

THE BATTLE IS THE LORD'S

The Battle is the Lord's

While speaking to His disciples on one occasion, Jesus told said that at some point in their lives, they would be faced with offense; not one, but many *(Luke 17:1).* One of the hardest and challenging commandments He gave to His disciples was to bless, love, and pray for those that trespass against them.

Human beings are created with an urge to hurt or harm the one who hurt them in return for an injury or wrong they suffered. It is part of human nature to seek revenge on the offending party. It is universally experienced by all cultures. Vengeance is a fruit of bitterness. If a person harbors thoughts of revenge, he can develop anxiety and act blindly through anger, rather than through reason. Revenge keeps the wound open and fresh; it does not bring healing. Instead, it causes a cycle of retaliation

As a believer you need to give God time and room to fight for you.

Jesus prayed and asked His Father to forgive all those who played a part in His death, because they didn't know what they were doing. Stephen prayed a similar prayer; he asked God to forgive those who were stoning him.

A prayer that leaves the matter in God's hand makes it impossible for bitterness to take root. When you know and are fully persuaded that God is going to act on your behalf, you rest in Him.

Beloved, do not avenge yourselves, but rather give place to wrath; for it is written, *"Vengeance is Mine, I will repay," says the Lord.* Romans 12:19, (NKJV).

A certain man (Edward), trusted his friend

(Nicholas) with a large sum of money, while they were trying to put up a business. Nicholas took the money and fled, going to a far country, leaving Edward with a massive debt to pay. When Edward realized that his friend had left with the money, he got so angry, but later he chose to leave the matter in God's hands instead of continuing with bitter exchanges on email. Edward forgave and forgot; he had no bitterness against Nicholas. He struggled to pay the debt. Five years down the line, a friend of Nicholas contacted Edward and informed him of how chaotic Nicholas' life had become. Edward realized how effective it is to leave room for God's wrath; He will avenge, He will repay.

Vengeance belongs to God; the battle is His.

Chapter Ten

FINAL WORD

Final Word

Life, without a doubt, is full of challenges, pain and agony. We live in a society that is full of suffering. We live at a time when there is overwhelming pressure from all spheres of life. Today, it's more likely that more than one thing will cause offense in your life. Life is becoming unbearable by the day, and the enemy is fighting believers harder, trying to devour them and strip them off the cover of God's love.

People have gone through suffering, betrayal, pain, loss and untold agony in marriage, business, career, ministry and other spheres. Consequently, many have picked seeds of offense which have over time germinated and developed roots of bitterness. That has led to an outbreak of cases of marital instability, breakdown of relationships, sicknesses and diseases, stress, suicide, homicide and many other ills in the society.

In spite of the apparent hopeless situation, God has worked out a way for those who love Him and have been called according to His purpose. God has poured out immeasurable grace upon His children to strengthen, heal and give hope to them all. Through the gift of His Word and His Son Jesus Christ, God has poured out His unfailing love to us. John 1:16 says that through Jesus, grace and truth was delivered to the world.

For from His fullness we have all received, grace upon grace. For the law was given through Moses; grace and truth came through Jesus Christ.

Jesus came so that we may receive the gift of freedom and redemption. Those whom He freed are free indeed.

So, if the Son sets you free, you will be free indeed. John 8:36 (NKJV).

Christ desires that the Word of God which He speaks into our lives brings the fullness of joy to us.

These things have I spoken unto you, that my joy might remain in you, and that your joy might be full. John 15:11 (NKJV).

God desires that nothing will hold us down in bondage, sin or away from His love. He desires that we overcome all the schemes that the enemy might use to rob us of the joy of God. When we get tempted or smitten (and this happens often), the Holy Spirit of God and the angels assigned over us minister encouragement, hope and healing to us. The Bible teaches that though a righteous man may fall seven times, the Lord will lift him up again.

For a righteous man may fall seven times and rise again. Proverbs 24:16(NKJV).

We are also encouraged not to allow offense or anger to take root in our hearts.

Be angry, and do not sin: do not let the sun go down on your wrath, nor give place to the devil. Ephesians 4:26-27(NKJV).

God has opened up a door of repentance to us all by which we may fall back to Him and regain a righteous stand.

Repent therefore and be converted, that your sins may be blotted out, so that times of refreshing may come from the presence of the Lord. Acts 3:19(NKJV).

2 Timothy 2:20-21 says:

In a great house there are not only vessels of gold and silver, but also of wood and clay, some for honor and some for dishonor. Therefore, if anyone cleanses himself from the latter, he will be a vessel for honor sanctified and useful for the Master, prepared for every good work.

I write to exhort you to follow the way of the Lord and remain in Him. My desire is that you will remain strongly rooted in His word and His love so that no offense or bitterness will edge you out. And even when you are tempted by offenses as it happens sometimes, you will remember that God still loves you and is willing to help you get up again. Strive hard not to allow offense to produce roots of bitterness or its fruits in your life, ministry, marriage, business or career. With the help of the Holy Spirit and the love of God, it is possible to overcome bitterness and live a fruitful life.

God bless you.

- END -